THE
GHOSTLY TALES
OF
THE
CATSKILLS

Published by Arcadia Children's Books
A Division of Arcadia Publishing
Charleston, SC
www.arcadiapublishing.com

Spooky America is a trademark of Arcadia Publishing, Inc.

First published 2023

Manufactured in the United States

ISBN: 978-1-4671-9731-1

Library of Congress Control Number: 2023931843

All images used courtesy of Shutterstock.com.

THE GHOSTLY TALES OF THE CATSKILLS

KAREN EMILY MILLER

Adapted from *Haunted Catskills* by Lisa LaMonica

TABLE OF CONTENTS & MAP KEY

Welcome to the Spooky Catskills!

You're in the Catskill Mountains on a ghost-hunting trip. You're stretched out on a blanket, enjoying the sun and the last of the warm breeze before the fall frost sets in. Closing your eyes, you imagine what this region of southeast New York might have been like twenty thousand years ago. You picture a glacier rising above you, a vast sheet of ice covering the whole region. As it travels, ever so slowly, it grinds and crushes mountains and forests.

Then you think of the Catskills, more recently, but still a long time ago. The ice is melting. You can almost hear the torrents of water, foaming and thundering across the land.

Where you lay, you watch the dusk deepen to night. That rush of water carved out the purple mountains, forests, fields, and meadows that change color as the sun sets.

This spot is so magical. So enchanted. Perhaps even haunted. It's the perfect place to tell a spooky tale—and then tell it again. Perhaps you've heard the stories of Rip Van Winkle and the Headless Horseman, some of the most famous Catskill legends. But do you know about the indigenous Romeo and Juliet or the Catskill Witch? The lesser-known ghost stories of the Catskills will have you on the edge of your seat. There are so many stories waiting for you. Read on . . . if you dare!

The Van Schaack House

At Kinderhook Village Green, most of the leaves have fallen. Even though there's no snow, it's cold. You're glad the Van Schaack Bed and Breakfast is close by. Within minutes, you and your parents are checking in. You wonder how close your room will be to the dining room. That's where the ghost of an American Revolutionary soldier is said to appear. Supposedly, there's no mistaking which side the spirit fought for. The ghost can't be a

British Soldier because those who see him say he's dressed in dark blue, maybe green. They are certain he doesn't like wearing red.

You and your parents have studied the history of the Van Schaack House. In this part of New York, the Americans had a rocky start during the Revolutionary War. The first skirmish (an unplanned battle) with the British ended in a draw, but both sides lost lives. Then the Americans rallied. During the next battle, they crushed the British troops and cut off British General Burgoyne's supply lines. Burgoyne surrendered.

After the win, the European enemies of England joined America in fighting. Things were looking up for America.

The proper gentlemen and ladies of the Van Schaack family invited the defeated Burgoyne to stay at their grand home. It was such an unexpected gesture of goodwill that a local wrote a song about it.

For the bold Burgoyne was marching,
With his thousands marching down,
To do battle with the people,
To do battle for the crown.
But Stark he lay at Bennington,
By the Hoosic's water's bright,
And Arnold and his forces,
Gathered thick on Bemis height.

You can guess what General Burgoyne thought when he came through the Van Schaack front door. With the entry hall's luxurious carpets and a two-story curving staircase, you have a feeling he'd feel right at home. You wonder, though, what a commoner might think. This is a home for the rich.

The manager shows you around the house. In the dining room, there's an open cupboard of dainty teacups and crystal glass. "They undoubtedly used their best silver for the general," he says.

Now you understand why an American soldier might make an appearance. Imagine life as a soldier: days without enough food, nights spent outdoors. Perhaps one of the soldiers had been assigned guard duty at the house. Imagine how he might have felt when he looked in the dining room window. He'd see his enemy sipping brandy in front of a warm fire. Some say that's why the soldier reportedly burst into the parlor.

You sit on one of the dining room chairs, hoping it will get dark soon. That's when the soldier's ghost is said to appear. You've read that he first appeared in 1942 during a dinner party. In your mind, you hear the glasses clinking and the scritch of silverware on china plates. You can hear the laughter and chitter-chatter of the guests.

Suddenly, the guests feel a cold wind. They turn to see what window might be open. What they see chills them more than the gust of winter wind. A shadow on the wall marches back and forth, back and forth. As they watch, the shadow solidifies into a figure of a man. Dressed in a Colonial uniform, he carries a musket on his shoulder. He seems to be both inside and outside the wall. After a time, he disappears. Was his ghostly guard duty finished for the night?

You decide to ask the owner to light the fire and serve drinks. Maybe this will recreate the scene that drew the ghost soldier into the house. But after an hour of waiting, no one has appeared—not the soldier or any of the bed and breakfast staff. You sigh. If you had arrived on September 24, the anniversary of the battle, you might have been able to see him.

Later, you can't help feeling a little disappointed as you drift off to sleep. But even if you can't see him, you feel safer knowing there *just* might be a ghostly solider keeping watch . . .

CHAPTER 2

Lindenwald

The next day, you and your parents take a guided tour of Lindenwald, the one-time beloved home of Martin Van Buren, the eighth president of the United States. The house is part of the Martin Van Buren State Park and National Historic Site. Built in 1797—more than two hundred and twenty-five years ago!—this place *must* have some ghosts lurking around. After all, Washington Irving, who wrote "The Legend of Sleepy Hollow," even lived here for a time. If you don't know that story, you're in for a doozy.

It's about a schoolmaster named Ichabod Crane who falls in love with Katrina, the daughter of the richest man in town. Unfortunately, Katrina already has a sweetheart. But Ichabod tries to win her affections anyway. One night, he proposes marriage to Katrina. She rejects him.

That was the start of a very bad night for Ichabod. Lost in his thoughts—and wondering how Katrina could have refused him—he's not paying attention to his surroundings. Another horseback traveler suddenly appears on the trail, surprising him. Ichabod jumps, for he's a timid man. Imagine how he felt when he saw that the man on the horse had no head!

It was the Headless Horseman, a Hessian soldier who had died in the American Revolutionary War while fighting on the side of the British. (The British were allies of his homeland, Hesse, now part of Germany.) To his horror, Ichabod guesses the soldier was killed by a cannonball that knocked his head off! Poor Ichabod spurs his horse and runs. It's only when he crosses the bridge that he begins to slow down. According to the stories, the horseman can't cross over water. Ichabod must have thought he was safe.

Poor Ichabod.

You shake your head as you remember what happens next.

The Headless Horseman reaches under his cloak and pulls out his bloody head. He throws it across the bridge, and it splats against *Ichabod's* head. Ichabod is knocked off his horse. The next morning, Ichabod's horse is found grazing outside his former lodging.

Ichabod, though, is never seen again.

Suddenly, your dad hands you the camera.

You jump a little, still thinking about the Headless Horseman.

"Will you get a picture of me by the Lindenwald sign?" he asks.

You nod yes and he starts to back up. But then he trips and accidentally bumps into one of the two marble slabs in front of the house.

"Are you hurt?" the tour guide calls, running over. When the guide sees that Dad is okay, he peeks around to check on the slabs of marble. "Did you damage them?" He bends over, making sure there's not a dent or scratch in sight.

"I don't think so," Dad says, dusting himself off.

The guide lets out a whoosh of relief. "Lucky for you—and lucky for us all—the stones haven't been damaged," he says.

You can tell from his voice there's something spooky about them.

"They might look like ordinary slabs to you," the guide says when he sees the quizzical look in your eyes. "But we think they're the original tombstones of Mr. and Mrs. Merwin, who once owned this house. If anyone moves or damages the stones, the Headless Horseman will return."

Your eyes go wide.

THE Headless Horseman?

You picture a goblin ghost astride a snorting wild-eyed horse. Like the story, the horseman wears a blue Hessian uniform but is missing his head. You can't imagine what someone looks like after his head is blown off by a cannonball, and frankly, you don't want to know.

Gulp.

You're excited to see some ghosts today, but the Headless Horseman is one ghost you definitely do NOT want to meet.

You and your family follow the tour guide

back up to the porch. While he hands out cups of delicious apple cider, he tells you this is where a boy, long ago, saw a figure he described as a "white mommy ghost" floating back and forth. Later, a relative of the boy identified the ghost. It turns out, long before the little boy ever visited the house, an elderly cousin had come to live with the family. The cousin claimed to have suffered from terrible aches and pains and spent most of her evenings outside on the porch. She said the cool breezes soothed her. And as the story goes, the breezes continued to soothe her . . . even *after* she passed away.

"From that point on," the tour guide says, "the little boy refused to step foot on this porch—*ever* again."

You can understand why the little boy stayed away. After all, a harmless ghost is still a ghost. Not everyone is as eager to meet one as you are.

You break away from the group to get a

better look around. The old porch creaks eerily below your feet as you walk, but—sadly—you don't see any ghostly lady floating anywhere.

In fact, you don't see any spirits at all.

Where *are* the ghosts of Lindenwald? According to rumors, there are a lot of them. One is supposed to be the son of Martin Van Buren. Another is Aaron Burr, the third American vice-president. A motley crew of ghost servants is supposed to haunt the house, too. There's a drunken butler who shows up from time to time. He's known for opening doors. There's also an angry cook who jumps out of the chimney. She's covered in ashes and her eyes burn with fire.

Suddenly, you see a flash of light from the corner of your eye. Could it be the ghost of the angry cook?! You spin around but quickly realize it's only the reflection of a passing car.

You can't help feeling a little disappointed.

Have all the ghosts left the building? Maybe they got bored haunting the same place for centuries and found somewhere else to lurk?

The group heads back inside and you trudge behind. But a few minutes before the tour ends, you *finally* get your reward for ghost hunting.

On the second floor, you notice your guide covertly shut one of the bedroom doors as he walks by. It seems like a strange thing to do, so you hide behind a chair and wait for him to go downstairs. Finally, he does. You scramble to your feet and run to the door. To your surprise, before your hand even reaches the knob, the door creaks open! You peek inside, but no one is there. You shut the door again, thinking maybe the tour guide didn't latch it properly. But a second later, the door opens *again*. Your heart starts to beat faster. Could this be . . . the ghost butler?

You decide to test it one last time. Slowly, you click the door shut, making sure it's *firmly* closed before letting go. After a few seconds, nothing happens.

Come on.

You stare at it hard, but again, the door still doesn't move.

Come ON.

You wait for what feels like an eternity . . . but nope. Nothing.

Finally, you let out a grumpy sigh. What a bust this ghost tour has been. You're about to head downstairs when you hear a soft, eerie sound that sends a shiver straight up your spine.

CREEEEAAAAAAAAK.

You freeze.

Slowly, you look up. Your mouth drops open—but then you grin.

The door is WIDE open.

And for a split second, you think maybe— just *maybe*—you see the ghostly butler, smiling right back at you.

CHAPTER 3

The Man with One Arm

TANNERSVILLE, NEW YORK

If you've ever gone to summer camp, you know scary stories are a camp tradition. Every night, whether inside the cabin or gathered with your bunkmates around a crackling campfire, the counselor scares you silly. One of the most famous stories is about a one-armed man. It's usually a lumberjack or a hook-handed killer. In the Catskills, it's a man who wants to *find* his arm.

As the story goes, the man roams the woods calling, "*Have you seen it?*"

(p.s. If you happen to hear him, that's your cue to run.)

One late autumn night, while you and your parents are camping near Lake Tremper, a short drive from Tannersville, New York, your dad retells the story. You angle your camp chair away from the fire, which spits red hot ashes every time the wind blows.

"Back in 1883," your dad begins, "everyone was excited when the railroads decided to link Tannersville to other towns in the Catskills. Running a railroad took a lot of men, so this meant work for the locals."

"What kind of work?" you ask.

"Oh, there were lots of jobs to fill," your dad says. "They needed conductors, engineers, porters, track workers, train station masters, you name it. But the track workers had perhaps the most important job. If the train ran on the wrong set of rails, it could crash into a train coming the other way. One train per track was the rule."

You try to imagine what it must have been like to be a railroad worker all those years ago. The conditions were probably really tough. Lots of long days and heavy lifting. Extreme weather conditions. Wild animals. Not to mention all the things that could potentially go wrong. Slips. Falls. Explosions. Fires. And of course. . . the dangers of the trains themselves.

"Later," your dad continues, "in 1933, the railroad needed repairs. One of the track workers was a brakeman named Hank. Depending on the destination, a train had to choose which track to follow. There could be as many as four choices. The brakeman knew when and where other trains ran. His job was to choose which set of railroad tracks to follow. To do so, he'd use a long lever to move the tracks back and forth. He also carried an axe just in case the switch was rusty and hard to move."

You scoot a little closer to the campfire. Something about the word "axe" makes you think the story might be taking a spooky turn.

"Hank's last night began like any other," your dad says. "The train chugged along until it reached the east side of Lake Tremper, where the tracks separated. Hank hopped off the train and went to pull the lever. Only, the lever didn't move. Thinking there might be something stuck, Hank leaned over and felt around under the track. But when he tried to pull his arm out, it wouldn't budge."

Your eyes go wide. "His arm was *stuck*?"

Your dad nods ominously.

"What happened next?" you ask. Even though you're scared you already know what he's going to say.

"After a while," your dad says, "Hank reached for his lantern. It was getting dark and he needed more light to see what was trapping his arm. But unfortunately, when he moved the lantern, the train engineer saw the light swaying back and forth."

You frown. "What does that mean?"

"Well, he thought Hank was signaling for him to move. How could he know Hank was lying down on the tracks, struggling to free his arm? The engineer got up steam and barreled down the tracks. And then..." Your dad shakes his head solemnly. "The train tore off Hank's arm."

"*What*?!" you exclaim. "What happened to him after that? Did he ... make it?"

"Some say Hank left his arm on the track," your dad replies. "They say he grabbed his axe and lantern and ran into the woods. But he was

clearly never the same. The mild-mannered brakeman had gone crazy with pain. He was now an axe-wielding maniac."

The fire crackles loudly and you jump a little in your camp chair. "*Maniac?*" you whisper, eyeing the dark woods all around you.

"That's right," your dad says. "Hank went on a rampage. That night, he struck the Conservation Camp. That was where the government workers who repaired park trails slept. It was during the Depression when jobs were scarce. The 150 men, so happy with finding work, slept peacefully. They had no idea what was coming through the forest. Survivors of the attack said Hank tore into camp and chopped off the left arms of eleven men."

"*Gross!*" you shout. "Did they arrest him?"

Dad shakes his head. "They never found Hank." He stands up. "Now, I have a surprise for you." He takes a couple of steps away from your campsite, then walks into the woods. Not too far, but deep enough for him to click on his flashlight. "They're over here," he calls. "These are the train tracks Hank worked on."

You and Mom look at each other. You know she doesn't want to go. Neither do you. But you can't stop yourselves.

With your feet crunching on twigs and fallen branches, you push your way through the undergrowth to the train tracks. Little trees have taken root and weeds run wild over the rails.

You stand silently, waiting. Dad aims his flashlight down the track. Mom clicks hers on and off, almost as if she's testing to make sure it works.

You stand on the tracks for what seems like an hour. Later, your parents say it only took a few minutes. But you felt like you were frozen when you saw a light making its way down the track toward you. It swung slowly from side to side.

"*Can you see it?*"

You freeze. Did that voice come from inside your head? Were you imagining it? Or . . .

"*Run!*" Dad yells suddenly.

You and your mom are already running. You stumble over logs, pick yourself up, and sprint back to your campsite. Dad douses the fire while you quickly fold up the tent and Mom packs the camp stove and pots and pans. A few minutes later—out of breath—the three of you pile into the car. You lock the doors, of course.

You've been back on the road for a while when you ask, "Did you hear him, too?"

Your mom and dad look at each other, then at you.

"I heard something," Mom admits.

"I thought it was you, asking if I saw the light," says Dad. "I also heard a rustle in the woods."

You shiver as you stare out the window, watching the spooky woods fly by. You remember your parents giving you advice last year before you went to summer camp.

Don't go into the woods alone at night.

Now you know why.

Vanderbilt House Hotel

PHILMONT, NEW YORK

You've probably heard the name Vanderbilt before. Cornelius Vanderbilt, the railroad builder, was one of the richest men in America in the 1800s.

You're surprised when your family pulls up to the Vanderbilt House Hotel in Philmont, New York. This house is nothing like the sprawling Biltmore Estate your parents took you to in Asheville, North Carolina. They told you this hotel would be smaller, but you didn't expect it to be *this* small. The Biltmore, the biggest private home in America, has thirty-five bedrooms. The Vanderbilt House Hotel only has eight.

"Why the name Vanderbilt?" you ask your parents. "The real Vanderbilts wouldn't stay here. It's way too small."

They explain that the hotel wasn't built for the family; it was built to house people who worked for the Vanderbilt railroads. The company was adding tracks to its line and providing a boarding house was a good idea. The house was across the street from the railroad itself. That way, the workers could easily go from one workplace to another.

Years later, Leverett Mansfield bought the boarding house and turned it into a hotel. The Mansfield family thrived, and so did the hotel. For a while, they left the running of the hotel to others. However, the Mansfields never forgot about it. Sixty years later, one of the Mansfield descendants bought it back from the last owner.

Mom stops the car. "We made it!" She almost jumps out of the car.

"She's excited about staying here," Dad explains. "She read the ghosts at Vanderbilt House Hotel are supposed to be friendly."

Friendly ghosts? You remember some of the stories you've heard about the Vanderbilt House Hotel. There's the ghost of a previous owner, who is said to haunt the hotel's bar and office. You recall your dad saying something about him liking popcorn and cigarettes. To this day, people still smell them from time to time.

Then there are the stories your mom has told you about the attic. Apparently, some guests were investigating the hotel and opened the attic door. They didn't see just one ghost—they saw three! And according to local stories, these guests weren't the last to see them.

Then there's the smell of men's cologne in one of the guest rooms. No matter how often the owners air out the room, the scent always comes back after a few days. Could it be the ghost of a Vanderbilt family member?

Oh, and you almost forgot about the ghost on the porch! People say he looks like he's waiting for a train. Except . . . the train stopped running years ago. The man doesn't seem to notice, though. He just leans back in his chair, smoking a cigarette and adjusting his cowboy hat. It's almost as if he's relaxing outside on a long-ago sunny day.

Suddenly, you realize you need to visit the bathroom. It's been a long drive. You can't wait for your parents to check into your room, so you rush inside to the lobby bathroom. You're in such a hurry, you don't notice the occupied sign on the door. When you push it open, you're surprised to see a white-haired woman standing at the sink. "Get out!" she yells at you.

"Sorry!" you cry as you dash out of there. But you can't stop thinking about her, even after finding another bathroom. She could have asked you nicely. There was also something odd about her, like she didn't belong in that bathroom either. Her long dress and straw hat looked like they came out of a history book. Could she have been one of the Vanderbilt's ghosts?

You rejoin your parents just in time to hear the manager say, "No, not *that* room. Last week, a guest saw the schoolteacher ghost dancing in the corner. Apparently, she kept them up all night."

Mom's smile disappears.

"Oh, that doesn't mean you won't see her," the manager reassures Mom. "She floats downstairs, too. She'll be wearing a filmy white dress." Then the manager leans over the desk and whispers, "Just don't be startled when you *do* see her. She doesn't have a head."

"Is there a ghost in the restroom?" you ask. She wasn't headless, but she *was* in a bad mood.

The manager chuckles. "She's grouchy, isn't she? She likes to have the bathroom to herself."

That afternoon, while Mom and Dad take a nap, you try out your new video game. But you can't concentrate. Someone is playing a game in the hallway—jacks, by the sound of it. You

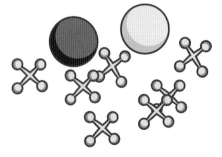

keep hearing the pong of a little bouncing ball and the clatter of jacks hitting the floor.

You get up from the couch and slowly open the door. You don't want to scare the kid away. You're just going to tell him to play somewhere else.

But weirdly, when you peer into the hallway, no one is there.

Huh?

You're sure someone was just playing jacks right here a second ago. You're about to go back into your room when a lady suddenly appears in the hall. You jump when you see her—you didn't see or hear any doors open or close. Dressed in a high-neck blouse with a long skirt, she looks very serious. She turns and glares, hands-on hips, like she's about to scold you. When your eyes meet hers, an icy chill runs right through you.

"Excuse me," you mutter quickly, and dart back inside your room.

Was she a GHOST?

The slam of the door wakes your parents. They decide it's time to eat dinner, but you're not sure you'll be able to eat. You're buzzing with too much excitment.

Then again, maybe you'll see another ghost or two in the dining room!

You follow your parents out of the room.

As you are about to walk downstairs, you see a portrait of a lady wearing a high-neck blouse. You do a double take—that's the same lady you just saw outside your room! "Who's that woman in the painting?" you ask your mom.

"I believe she's one of the early owners of the hotel," says Mom. "Supposedly, their spirits are still hanging around."

"I think I've already met three of them," you mumble under your breath.

"Hey!" Mom laughs. "Save some ghosts for us."

You look around the dining room. Everyone must have already eaten because you three are the only guests.

The waiter looks pale and sickly, almost as if he has the stomach flu. He taps his foot impatiently as you sit for dinner. Maybe he wants to go home to bed.

When he notices you watching him, he explains himself. "I'm sorry. I'm a little upset. I started work last week and ever since, strange things have been happening to me. Each time I'm in the kitchen, I see a little boy peeking at me through the window. I'll run into the dining room to catch him, but he's never there."

You and your parents exchange glances. Could this little boy be yet *another* ghost?

After he takes your order, the waiter adds, "That's not all. Today, the chef yelled at me for no reason. He said I turned up the heat on the kitchen burners and spoiled the soup. I saw the flames, too—they were higher than the pots! I thought the chef must have turned them up by mistake." He sighs. "I was turning them *down* when he walked back into the kitchen."

That's when you hear a rap on the kitchen door. You turn swiftly, but this time, there's nothing paranormal about it. It's the chef, gesturing to the waiter.

The waiter turns even paler. "He must be ready to close the kitchen. I'll charge the dinner bill to your hotel room." He flips the order pad shut and looks around the dining room nervously. "I don't like to be here alone. There's always someone watching me." He shakes his head. "But when I look, I never see anything."

Later that night, when you're tucked

into bed, you can't help replaying what the waiter said.

There's always someone watching . . .

Could there by someone watching you . . . *now*? You wait up as long as you can in case of anything spooky, but nothing strange happens. Still, as your eyelids grow heavy, you can't help but feel proud. You saw *three* of the Vanderbilt House Hotel ghosts in ONE afternoon!

For a kid ghost hunter—or *any* ghost hunter, for that matter—that's pretty darn spooktacular.

Captain's Inn,
Point Lookout

EAST WINDHAM, NEW YORK

Picture yourself standing atop an observation tower about two thousand feet above sea level. As you slowly look around, you can see five states: Vermont, New Hampshire, Massachusetts, Connecticut, and New York. An amazing sight! You stay up on the tower, even though the wind is freezing cold. There's simply so much to see, from brilliant fall leaves to pumpkin patches to sprawling cornfield mazes.

(Later, you're not surprised when you start to feel a cold coming on.)

Your family is in East Windham for the night. Since the fall tourist season is winding down, your parents were able to book a room at the Captain's Inn at Point Lookout. You're already excited to be staying at the inn, but when you find out you're all staying in Room 12, you're *really* excited.

After all, you've heard some pretty spooky stories about Room 12.

Your parents notice you coughing and tell you to stay in the room while they go to supper. They promise to bring something back for you to eat. You can't believe your luck. Now you can ghost hunt by yourself!

You're about to put on your sneakers so you can *sneak* up on spirits when the housekeeper comes into the room for turndown service.

"Are you enjoying your stay in Room 12?" she asks. "It's famous, you know." She puts two wrapped chocolates on Mom's and Dad's pillows, then hands you three. Then she lowers her voice. "Will your parents mind if I tell you a ghost story?"

You tell her that your parents *love* ghost stories. In fact, the spookier the better.

She sits down at the desk and begins. "I'm not sure when the hauntings started. When

Ron and Laurie, the owners, bought the inn, they knew it needed renovation. But they had no idea about anything paranormal. A fire had destroyed the original building, which was said to be quite grand. But business had been bad for a while. Ron and Laurie were the sixth owners in just twelve years."

"Isn't that a lot of owners?" you ask.

The housekeeper nods. "They probably should've known something odd was going on, but Ron and Laurie were so excited about buying the inn that they ignored all the hints. Even when their cat, always a calm soul, started acting strangely, they thought it was because they had moved to a new place. When Laurie went into Room 12, the cat refused to go with her. I guess they didn't know that animals and children are especially sensitive to the paranormal."

"*I'm* still technically a child . . ." you trail off. "I don't turn thirteen until next year. Am I young enough to see one?"

The housekeeper smiles. "You might be one of the lucky ones." She gives you an appraising look, as if she's measuring your courage. "Or, one of the *unlucky* ones who have stayed in Room 12."

She continues. "Ron and Laurie's first clue that something was wrong was the smell in this room. Not anywhere else in the inn, just here."

You sniff the air. It smells okay to you. Just like air freshener and furniture polish.

"Have you ever smelled a dead mouse?" she asks.

You think back and recall a time your cat hid a dead mouse under your couch. It smelled like rotten cabbage. Pew! It was *putrid*! "Yes," you say, grimacing. "I know the smell."

"The owners thought it was a mouse, too," she says. "They called exterminators, then special house cleaners, but nothing worked. Finally, they gutted the bedroom. After they stripped it down to the wall studs, the smell disappeared for a while. Still, the other housekeepers and I knew there was something wrong with the room. Lights flickered on and off and so did the television. But every time we checked . . . nobody was there."

The housekeeper glances at her watch. "I still have time before I have to turn down the beds in the other rooms. Anyway, I've often felt a cold breeze when I walked by your room. I've seen shadows in the hall." She shakes her head. "I'm glad that's all *I've* felt."

"What about other people who work here?" you ask. "Have they felt things, too?"

She nods. "One of the waitresses had a real paranormal experience. She had been staying in this exact room, which was empty at the time, and thought she was lucky since she just had to walk down a few steps to get to work. One night, though, her luck turned. The restaurant had closed, and she went to her room, Room 12. Suddenly, she felt a heaviness, a feeling of unbearable grief. She got out of bed, opened the door, and found herself face-to-face with a woman dressed in a flowing white gown. The waitress had heard smells can trigger powerful memories and emotions, so at first she'd wondered if the woman in white was giving off some kind of smell that

made her think of sad things. But then . . ." the housekeeper trails off.

"Then what?" you prod when she doesn't immediately finish her sentence.

"Then she saw a woman . . . floating *in the air*! She was a tiny thing with long flowing hair. The waitress ran downstairs to tell Ron and Laurie what had happened. After that, she packed her bags and left."

Whoa. You look around the room slowly. You can feel the tiny hairs on the back of your neck starting to stand up. Could the woman in white still be close by?

"Do you want to hear more?" the housekeeper asks. "Or have you had enough?"

Your chest feels a little jittery but you tell her you want to hear more.

"Room 12 was quiet for some time," she goes on. "After what happened to the waitress, Ron and Laurie decided to keep the room empty.

One night, though, the inn was so crowded that there was only one room left."

Your eyes go wide. "Was it . . . Room 12?"

"Sure was." She nods. "After a man checked in, everyone on staff waited for something to happen. At first, the night went on as usual, so everyone went to sleep. Then it became early morning. And that's when we first heard the screaming."

Your eyes grow wide. *"Screaming?"* you whisper.

"Yes. It was *awful*, like someone was being murdered! When we let ourselves in, we saw the guest running around the room, bumping into the bed and desk. He kept screaming about a terrible smell—but when Ron and Laurie tried to get him to leave the room, he refused! It's like he'd gone out of his mind. Eventually, they called 9-1-1 and the police got him under control."

You almost can't believe what you're hearing. Did all these things *really* happen? Or is the housekeeper just trying to scare you because you're a kid?

"Ron and Laurie called the PPA after that," she says.

"What's the PPA?" you ask.

"Pennsylvania Paranormal Association," she replies. "When the team came to investigate, they, too, felt a heaviness—an intense sorrow—right here in Room 12. They also smelled a rancid odor. The team's psychic said there was a female spirit trapped inside the room. They said she was upset, agitated, and almost in a state of frenzy. Each time they went into Room 12, their electromagnetic frequency detector, or EMF, *spiked*. And the smell"—she makes a face—"only got worse. Sometimes, it was hard to be in there without gagging."

She goes on to explain that EMF detectors

measure changes in the electromagnetic field—and that the frequency rises when a paranormal spirit is near—but you already knew that. You're a ghost hunter!

"Why do think the ghost was so upset?" you ask.

"The owners asked the police if there had been a death at the inn," the housekeeper answers, "but they never found any record of one. Later, a local told them that records had been lost when the town hall burned down years ago. So, there might have been a death that no one remembered."

You blink. "So, they never figured out what happened to her?"

The housekeeper gives you a knowing look. "The mystery lasted until a local lady stopped by with a story. As a child, she had heard about a death at the inn. A man and woman had checked in together, but the man left almost immediately. The man told the staff that the woman was ill, so he didn't want them to disturb her. They didn't, not for a week."

You start to get a bad feeling as she's telling the story. You sniff the air but your nose is too stuffy to detect any smells—strange or otherwise. "What happened to the woman?" you ask, though something tells you that you already know the answer.

"When they found her," the housekeeper says, "she was on the bed in a white nightgown. Sadly, she was dead."

A chill shoots up your spine.

"Ron and Laurie called back the PPA. This time the team brought cadaver and control dogs."

You nod. You've read that normal dogs aren't trained to detect death, but cadaver dogs are.

"The cadaver dogs went immediately to the

corner of the room," she says. "The same *exact* spot the psychic had predicted."

Your jaw drops. "Wow!"

The housekeeper lowers her voice. "There's *more*. One of the PPA team was sitting directly outside the kitchen. The door had little square glass windows so he could see inside. He noticed a small clock hanging on a wall. Suddenly, something passed in front of the clock, blocking it from her sight. She couldn't tell what it was, only that something had obstructed her view of the clock. Whatever it was, it went back and forth in front of the clock several times."

"Did they figure out what it was?" you ask.

She shakes her head. "When a team member was called into investigate, he couldn't see anything strange. The rest of the team left after a while, but not without experiencing the paranormal. They all saw shadows, felt cold spots, and had the feeling that someone—or *something*—was watching them."

You're barely aware that you've pulled the blanket up to your chin.

"Don't worry," the housekeeper tells you. "The psychic and the Pennsylvania Paranormal Association called in more experts. They performed a blessing ritual. It's done to cleanse a space and help a spirit cross over. Sometimes, a spirit will get stuck in our world and need help to leave."

"Did it work?" you ask.

The housekeeper gathers up the extra towels and soap. "I wouldn't be in this room if it hadn't."

The door opens suddenly and you and the housekeeper both jump. You turn and see your parents walk in with a covered bowl and packets of crackers.

"This is chicken soup." Mom puts it on the

desk. "The chef said it will cure anything that ails you."

The housekeeper leaves and you take a hot, delicious spoonful of soup. In an instant, it soothes your throat and clears your nose. You're happy your nose is working again and inhale deeply. What do you smell? The onions in the chicken soup, for one. The roses in your mom's perfume. You sniff a few more times, but nope. Nothing spooky.

Hmm. Maybe the cleansing ritual really DID work.

After finishing your soup, you lay down. As you drift off to sleep, you think about all the housekeeper's stories and how you can't *wait* to tell your friends that you've slept in a formerly haunted room. But suddenly, your eyes open. You sniff the air once, and then twice.

Wait a second. Are you dreaming? Or is that . . . rotten cabbage?

CHAPTER 6

The James and Lydia Canning Fuller House

SKANEATELES, NEW YORK

Your family's road trip to the Catskills has been fun (you've even seen some actual ghosts!), but maybe not *quite* as scary as you've hoped. You hope your paranormal luck will change.

You're ready for something REALLY spooky.

So when your parents pull into the parking lot of a church cemetery, you can't help feeling excited. Cemeteries are the *perfect* place to look for ghosts! From creepy statues and old mausoleums to haunted headstones and moonlit tombs, they're basically a ghost hunter's paradise.

When your parents park, you practically jump out of the car and head straight through the ivy-covered gates toward a crumbling angel statue that looks promising. "Hey!" you call to your mom and dad. "Over here!"

But they're not listening to you.

"It's somewhere around here," you hear your mom say to your dad as they walk up and down a row of headstones.

You frown. What is she looking for?

When you walk over, your mom explains that she's trying to find a grave marker that's shaped like a miniature coffin. There look to be many grave markers, but after a while, Mom calls out that she's found it.

You walk over and examine it. It does look just like a small coffin, only made of stone, not wood. It sits on top of the ground instead of underneath. You ask why this tombstone is different from the other ones in the graveyard.

More importantly, why should you care?

Your dad tells you this tombstone marker is special because it was used to mark the tunnel entrance to the Underground Railroad. It looked different from most tombstones, but not *too* different. The people who put it there didn't want to arouse suspicions. He explains that the Underground Railroad was a network of safe houses that people used to escape from enslavement before the Civil War.

"People known as abolitionists developed this network in secret," he says. "It was extremely dangerous for enslaved people to try to escape from their bondage. It was dangerous for people to help them, too. If abolitionists were caught, they could be fined or jailed."

 The tombstone's cover was just big enough for a man or woman to squeeze through. After they climbed in and replaced the

lid, they'd follow the tunnel to a house or church nearby.

You say, "I thought the Underground Railroad was above ground."

Your dad says tunnels were necessary if the safe houses or churches were in public places.

You look at the tombstone again. It isn't very large. How could anyone fit in there?

"The tunnels weren't often used," says Dad, "because they were dangerous. They were small—just big enough to crawl through. Any moment the ceiling or walls could collapse."

You remember learning in school that one hundred thousand people fled to freedom using the Underground Railroad. They must have taken many risks and faced many dangers.

Maybe that's why you're at a cemetery. This isn't a place anyone would go seeking the living.

You follow your parents as they cross the cemetery to a two-story white clapboard house. It looks like other houses in the neighborhood, though you see a historical marker in front of it. You take a closer look and read: *the James and Lydia Canning Fuller House.*

Your mom tells you the story of the house. At first, it drew attention because it was a station on the Underground Railroad. Then, about twenty years ago, strange things began to happen here as well. That's when ghosthunters took an interest.

One night, after the owner of the house (a woman named Regina) went to bed, she and her dog Lady met a ghost. First, Lady nosed Regina awake, and then Regina watched as Lady sniffed around the bedroom. Finally, the dog sat down in front of the bedroom closet and began making panicky little *woofs.* Lady wouldn't move and soon, Regina felt the hairs on her arm stand up.

Had a bat gotten into the house? Could it be a raccoon or squirrel? The house was over two hundred years old. Maybe there were holes in the attic?

Telling Lady to stay, just in case she needed protection, Regina slowly opened the closet door. What she saw, she would never forget: A woman was crouched in the back of the closet. Dressed like she was from the 1800s, the woman had wrapped her arms around her knees, almost as if trying to make herself too small to see.

Regina was surprised, but she wasn't afraid. She had lived in the house for over twenty years, so she knew its history. Two famous abolitionists, James and Lydia Canning, had built the house to be a station on the

Underground Railroad. This meant they'd also built a tunnel from the cemetery to their house. Had this ghost followed the very same tunnel?

After Regina reported her ghost sighting to the Underground Railroad's historical society, she was told that ghosts weren't new to the house. The spirit in the closet was her first, but probably not her last. In fact, they seemed certain she could expect more.

As it turned out, Regina *did* meet more ghosts over the years. Sometimes, she heard footsteps where no one was walking. Other times, she saw a face in the window.

After a while, Regina grew used to the spirits. When her daughter Amanda had a frightening experience, though, Amanda called in ghost-hunting experts. According to Regina, Amanda and a friend had been sitting on the porch and enjoying the evening air. Suddenly, a six-foot-tall man walked past them and then dissolved into the front of the house. They couldn't describe him well. It had happened so fast!

The Atlantic Paranormal Society (otherwise known as TAPS), came to investigate. Armed with night vision cameras, electronic voice phenomena recorders, and more, they spent a week at the Canning House. Though they couldn't find any hard evidence, they *did* discover some tantalizing hints.

While exploring the basement, a marble, or some other sphere, rolled past their feet. When they reviewed the film they'd taken during their stay, they saw a strange orb of light bob up and down in the air.

The paranormal investigators thought two kinds of spirits haunted the Canning House. One type were spirits who simply repeated everyday routines of their past life. They didn't seem aware of the living. In fact, they never interacted with them.

The second type were spirits who, for some reason, had become attached to the house. Had they died or experienced a tragedy there? Is that why they'd never left?

Standing outside the Canning House, you watch cars pass and people stroll by. It looks so peaceful. Maybe the Canning House is an example of a quiet haunting. After all, Regina says she has never felt afraid.

You look back across the street to the cemetery. What had it been like to creep underground to the trapdoor? You picture yourself crawling through a dirt tunnel on the way to a safe house. You hope the wood supports will hold up under the weight of the earth above. Then you imagine yourself, heart pounding as you tap on a trapdoor. You wait. Will someone answer your knock? You hope so. But what if the family has left home?

Or worse, what if they've been arrested?

Suddenly, you realize you've been holding your breath. You're lightheaded and your pulse is racing. What a reaction for someone who is only *imagining* what it was like to flee into the unknown in search of freedom. That must have taken REAL courage.

You wonder what it would be like if you could communicate with one of them. For a second, you try to lift the lid of the coffin-shaped tombstone. It doesn't budge, not even an inch. Maybe it's for the better, you realize. The idea of the tunnel is scarier than any ghost.

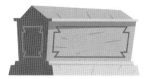

CHAPTER 7

Spook Rock

Columbia County, New York

You're the first to see the big boulder. Last night it snowed—early, for the season—so the rock is almost hidden under a blanket of white.

Your parents are discussing the next spot on the ghost tour and don't notice that you've run ahead. You grab a long branch with lots of twigs. It almost looks like a timber toothbrush, something the legendary giant lumberjack Paul Bunyan might have used.

The rock sits in Claverack Creek, but it's close enough to shore that you can brush off the snow. You're finished by the time Mom and Dad join you.

"I see you found Spook Rock," says Dad. "I've heard so many stories about this spot, I don't know which ones to believe."

"I know them all," you say proudly, puffing out your chest. You read the tourist brochures and searched the internet. You stayed up past midnight. You were sleepy, but it was worth it. Now, it's *your* turn to tell the ghost stories around here.

You clear your throat and use your serious voice, the one you imagine a professor might use. On this trip, you've heard plenty of people tell the tales. You know how to do it.

"Henry Hudson," you begin, "the English explorer, was looking for a shortcut to China. Travelers and storytellers told of an open water passage that linked the Atlantic to the Pacific Ocean. The only problem was . . . how to find it."

You go on to tell them how Hudson was just one of many looking for the new passage. Since the waterway was rumored to be above the Arctic Circle, Hudson concentrated many of his explorations in what is now upper New York state.

"In 1609," you say, "Hudson made his way to what is now Stockport, New York. He'd sailed into Upper New York Bay, then traveled by canoe up the Hudson River. Both the Hudson River and the city of Hudson are named for him." You grin. "Some people even say his

ghost still haunts the Catskills to this day . . ."

"Can we get to the Spooky Rock part, please?" Mom asks. "It's cold, honey. And it's getting late."

You sigh. Mom can be very impatient. But you can't deny she's right. Even though it's still technically fall, snow and ice already blanket the creek.

"*Spook Rock*," you correct Mom. "Not Spooky Rock. Basically, the story of Spook Rock is a story of girl meets boy. There are a bunch of different versions, but in this one, the daughter of a Mohican chief fell in love. Spoiled and protected her whole life, she wasn't used to being told 'No.' Her father had given her everything she ever wanted, but not, as it turns out, the boy she wanted to marry. The boy was the son of a chief from a neighboring village. How they met, no one knows. But they did and they fell in love."

You shake your head. "Unfortunately, the girl's tribe and the boy's tribe were enemies. The girl's father forbade any contact between the two. But the girl didn't listen. She couldn't bear being apart from her boyfriend. So, one night, when the village had settled down to sleep, she ran away."

Your parents exchange a worried glance.

"She had broken one of the most important rules of the Mohican People," you say. "She had disobeyed a parent. Little did she know, the Great Spirit was watching. And he was *not* pleased."

"What happened next?" your dad asks.

"The girl didn't think about angering the Great Spirit. Neither did her boyfriend. One night, they met at their usual spot, on a large cliffside boulder. They vowed they would always be together, no matter who tried to stop them. The Great Spirit spewed out torrents of rain and filled the sky with rolling thunder. The girl and boy clung to each other, waiting for the storm to pass." You pause. "It didn't. The Great Spirit threw down a lightning bolt so powerful that it catapulted the boulder off the cliff."

"Did they . . . make it?" Mom asks.

You shake your head. "The couple fell with the boulder. Even if they had survived the fall, they wouldn't have escaped. The boulder pinned them underwater."

You suppose, in a terrible way, the girl and boy got their wish.

Together forever.

"Look carefully," you say. "Is the rock moving? People say that when the Claverack Church bells ring, the rock will roll over and free them." You shiver a little and stick your hands in your pockets. It really is cold out. But you can't leave. Not yet.

"A Mohican descendant says that's the wrong story," you explain. "It's still a girl-meets-boy scenario, but this time, the girl is a Dutch settler whose family settled near a Mohican village. At first, the Dutch adults allowed the boy and girl to see each other. They never dreamed they would fall in love. How could they? They were from such different backgrounds."

"Uh-oh," Mom says. "I've got a bad feeling I know where this is going."

"When the Dutch elders realized the two wanted to marry," you continue, "they forbade the boy to enter the settlement. The poor boy was brokenhearted. He left the settlement and his village behind and struck off into the woods. He wandered for days. He had no food or shelter, but he didn't care. He grew weaker and weaker. One day he came to a cliff over the Claverack Creek. Thinking he had nothing to live for, he threw himself over the edge and died on the rocks below."

Dad winces. "Is that the spookiest version of the story?"

"No," you reply, "I think it's this next one. A girl from a Dutch settlement falls in love with a Mohican boy."

"That sounds the same," interrupts your mom.

You ignore her and keep going. It *is* different from the others.

"Like the second story I told you, it's the Dutch settlers who don't approve of the match. One night, the Dutch girl and Mohican boy snuck off into the woods. They met at their favorite place, the boulder above Claverack Creek. They thought they were alone, but they weren't. A group of Dutchmen, armed with muskets, killed the boy and the girl."

For a moment, there's no sound but the whisper of the wind through the snowy trees.

"Okay." Your mom shivers. "I think I'm ready to go now. It's *freezing*."

She doesn't realize the next part of your story might make her forget all about the cold.

You glance up at the sky. You just need to wait until the moon rises. It needs to be dark enough to see shadows. The good news it, it's almost winter, so the sun sets early. "Just a little longer," you tell them. "Trust me. It'll be worth it."

When the shadows of the trees grow sharp, you tramp back to the rock. Suddenly, church bells begin to toll in the distance. You pause to listen, their melody soft and spooky.

Perfect timing.

"Look!" You point to the rock. "The shadows of the boy and girl should appear. That's what the legend says. When the bells of Claverack Church ring, the boulder will roll over and release the girl and boy."

You and your parents watch and wait, but you don't see any shadows that look human. The rock hasn't moved. However, you *do* hear screams. Lots and LOTS of screams.

"What is that?!" your mom exclaims.

Your dad thinks the screams could be coming from a cougar trying to attract a mate. Except, according to guidebooks you've read, there *aren't* any cougars left in this part of New

York State. Could the sounds be something
else? Something . . . otherworldly?

Whatever they are, the shrieks send you all
back to the car.

And *fast*.

On the way back to Hudson, you can't help
replaying the sound in your head. Could it
really have been a mountain lion you heard?
Or . . . could the screams have been from a
ghostly girl who'd seen her lover killed?

To you, it had sounded like a heartbroken
woman.

As the road curves gently through the trees
and the sun sets over the spooky Catskills,
you're certain: it was no mountain lion.

You heard the spirit of the Dutch girl.

Rip Van Winkle House and Rip's Rock

ROUND TOP, NEW YORK

Whoosh! You're on a snowmobile, plowing through last night's snow on the trail. You didn't expect a winter wonderland in late November, but you'll take it—you love riding this thing! Using orange trail markers, you roar up to the spot you've been looking for: the GPS coordinates for the foundation of the Rip Van Winkle House.

Rip Van Winkle was make believe. Still, most people around here know his story. The main character in a famous short story by Washington Irving, Rip Van Winkle is the lazy bones in the Catskills who went into the mountains and took a twenty-year nap. After Irving became famous, a local built a rest stop and named it "The Rip Van Winkle House." Later, someone carved "Rip's Rock" into a big boulder nearby. People say the name Rip Van Winkle brought in lots of customers.

It's fun to use your orienteering skills. However, when you get to the spot, there's no house, just a layer of snow. But you're not discouraged. You know where to look. You clomp up a hill, look to the left, and there it is: a big boulder named "Rip's Rock." You've got your snowmobiling suit on to keep warm, so you pretend to be Rip Van Winkle while you wait for Mom and Dad. You sit down next to the rock and close your eyes.

"Trying to take a twenty-year nap?" your dad calls out when he and Mom catch up with you.

He sits down next to Mom on a log. Twisting open the top of the thermos, Dad pours hot chocolate into cups.

"Here's a new story about Rip Van Winkle," he says.

You're doubtful it's new. You already know the story. Rip, trying to avoid work, wandered off with his hunting dog, Wolf. He forgot all about hunting when he saw a big boulder covered with moss. It looked very cozy and inviting, so he propped himself up against a boulder to nap. But later, when he awoke, he discovered he had been asleep for twenty years!

"This is more a story about Rip's *friend,*

Solomon Brink," Dad explains. "The two of them were quite a pair. While Rip liked to think about something but never do it, Solomon jumped into action without taking time to think! That's what got them into trouble."

Your dad tells you that Solomon and Rip liked to hunt together. Rip usually napped or smoked his pipe. Solomon would run off into the woods, shooting his musket at anything that moved.

One day, Solomon announced he was going to kill a bobcat. He led Rip to a waterfall about four stories high. "This is the place," he told Rip. "The bobcat's up there."

Rip looked at the boulders he'd have to climb and said, "Why don't we wait down here? A bobcat's just as likely to come here for a drink."

Solomon snorted. "You can see for yourself, Rip. There's no bobcat here."

Rip had to agree.

It took an afternoon of pushing and poking for Solomon to get Rip to the top of the waterfall. When they finally got there, they saw a huge bobcat!

Wolf hid behind Rip's legs and whined. Solomon raised his musket, aimed, and fired.

Boom! Solomon's shot filled the air with smoke. But when the smoke cleared, the bobcat was gone. In the same place, the *exact spot* where the bobcat had been, now stood a buck deer. It was so big that its antlers must have gotten stuck in tree branches when it ran through the woods. The buck turned its head and looked at Solomon and Rip. To their surprise, it smiled at them!

Rip had never seen a deer smile before. He didn't even know they *could* smile!

A moment later, the buck bounded off into the woods. This time, Solomon didn't have to scold Rip into following him. He'd never been that deep in the forest before. It would be better to face the next surprise with Solomon by his side.

They followed the sounds of crackling branches, squawking birds, and *kuk-kukking* of squirrels. After a heart-thumping chase, Solomon stopped. "Do you see that clump of trees?" he whispered, pointing to a thicket where all the leaves had fallen. "He's in there, hiding. Look, you can see his antlers in the leaves." Solomon scooped gunpowder out of his leather pouch and loaded his musket.

"*Boom!*"

Solomon shouldered his musket and charged through the trees.

Rip and Wolf considered going after the

deer. Then they thought better of it. Rip was glad he did, for suddenly he heard a thundering crash. A big black bear burst out of the bushes where the buck had been! Rip was so startled, he dropped his musket. Wolf went on alert, his fur bristling and teeth bared. Neither one gave chase. The bear stopped a few yards away. Its distinctive scent—a mix of scat (that's bear poop), decay, and very bad breath—made Rip's eyes water. But even with tears in his eyes, he could still see what happened next plain as day: the bear *smiled* at him.

When Solomon returned, he asked, "Did you see that bear smile?"

Rip nodded. "That's bad magic. We'd better get out of these woods before we get into trouble."

Solomon laughed. "I'm not

afraid! Even if it's the Catskill Witch, I can handle her."

Rip gulped. "The Catskill Witch? The one who casts spells and puts curses on people?"

Solomon patted Rip on the shoulder. "Don't worry, Rip. Have I ever taken you into danger before?"

Plenty of times, Rip thought to himself. But Solomon was his friend, so he picked up his musket and followed. They explored every shadow in the woods, looked in caves, even stuck their muskets into piles of leaves. Nothing. Finally, they came to a rock fall. There were moss-covered boulders so big, they couldn't see over them.

"See that rock over there?" Solomon said  in a low voice. "It just sprouted bear ears." He aimed his musket and shot. Rip jumped in surprise when a red fox darted out and scampered past him. But this time, he *wasn't* surprised when the fox smiled at him.

It was nearing sunset when Solomon and Rip came to a clearing in the woods. Once again Solomon spotted something. "There! Look at those barberry bushes!"

Rip looked and saw the long snout and bright eyes of a fox peeking at them through the bushes. He said, "I'm not going in there. The thorns hurt! Just wait for it to come out."

Solomon didn't listen. He loaded his musket, aimed, and shot.

Boom.

A cloud of smoke filled the air. When it cleared a moment later, there stood the Catskill Witch. Hands on her hips and a snarl on her lips, she glared at them both.

Rip darted behind a tree and hissed at Solomon to join him. "Hurry! Maybe she'll forget about us if she can't see us."

But Solomon was spellbound. He stood as if frozen in place, staring into the witch's eyes. She didn't smile, or blink, or say a single word. Finally, she brushed by Solomon and walked into the woods.

"Let's go," Rip pleaded once the witch had disappeared. "*Please?*"

As usual, Solomon acted impulsively. "I'm going to catch her, Rip," he said. "I'm going to *show her* what happens when you play tricks on Solomon Blunt." With that, he marched off after the witch.

For a long while, Rip sat and smoked his pipe. Finally, he stood up. He couldn't let his best friend fight the witch alone. It was easy enough to pick up the trail. Withered leaves, dead birds, and trampled grass—all signs the witch and Solomon had passed through. Rip trudged up the mountain, afraid of what he might find. Finally, he saw Solomon, too far away to hear, but within sight.

Thunder rumbled. Black clouds gathered. At the very top of the mountain, Solomon disappeared into one of the black clouds. Rip ran, maybe for the first time in his life, and saw Solomon entering a cave.

There sat the witch, spinning storm clouds. She examined the black wisps as she worked. Rip saw that every once in a while, she'd gather up a cloud and fling it into the sky. She also had a pile of gourds next to her that she'd toss outside the cave onto the rocks. When one crashed, it let loose torrents of water.

Rip could just make out the words of the song she sang.

Blow, blow winds of ice,
Down the mountain pass;
Thunder and lightning
Rumble and roar,

And darkness fill the air
Till gone is all weather fair."

Then she looked at Solomon and smiled. "You've come for your trophy, have you?"

Picking up a gourd, she said, "Here it is!" She smashed the gourd on the floor of the cave. Up rose a swirling spring so large it carried Solomon out of the cave and over the edge of the cliff! Solomon fell 250 feet to the rocks below.

In that instant, Rip knew he wouldn't be hunting with Solomon anymore.

Rip scrambled down the mountain to the spot where he thought Solomon must lay.

To his surprise, a stream now rushed past where Solomon should have been.

"Over the years," Dad says, "Rip returned many times to that spot. He never found Solomon, but the stream remained."

"The locals named it Catskill Creek," Mom

chimes in. "It flows to this day." She puts down her cup of hot chocolate and points past the boulder. "That's the same creek, right over there."

Suddenly, Dad looks startled and jumps up. "*Hey!*" he cries. "Did you see that?"

You turn swiftly and spot the tail of a fox swish out from behind a tree. It couldn't have been more than twenty feet away. Your eyes go wide as you remember the sequence of transformations in Solomon's story: bobcat, buck, bear, fox, and finally . . . the Catskill Witch.

You gulp. Judging by your parents' expressions, they remember, too. You're not sure you believe in the Catskill Witch . . . but you jump back on your snowmobiles and whoosh away.

Just in case.

Caroline Sutherland's Corpse

CHATHAM, NEW YORK

You're headed home after your adventure in the Catskills. It's been a great trip, even if some of the ghosts have evaded you. When you pass the Chatham Center Cemetery, your mom stops the car.

There's one last gravesite she wants to find. The woman buried there is named Caroline Sutherland. She's not known for bravery or generosity. She's not known because she committed terrible deeds. Caroline Sutherland is famous because her dead body did not decay.

None of you know where the gravesite is. Still, you spend the morning looking for it. As you search, your dad begins to tell the spooky tale.

"Caroline Sutherland was a rich and beautiful girl." Dad pulls out a guidebook of local hauntings and opens it to a page with a girl's photo. "She does look like she was stylish," he says. "That hairdo was considered very fashionable in the 1850s."

You look at the girl's hair. It's wound and pinned so the sides look like English muffins.

Dad says, "Caroline led a charmed life. A year after this picture was taken, she met, married, and became pregnant. What luck, people must have said." He shakes his head. "But it wasn't lucky for her. Caroline died in childbirth. Even though she was dead, there was one last picture to be taken: her *death* portrait. Death portraits were the rage in the 1850s. A picture of a loved one was something the family could look at and remember."

You look at the death portrait. It feels kinda creepy knowing Caroline is dead in the picture, but at the same time, there's something almost peaceful about it. Wearing an off-white dress, her hair spread out on a pillow, she looks as if she's sleeping.

The family held a funeral in Illinois, where Caroline had been living with her new husband. But after that, her body and that of her stillborn baby were to be shipped to her childhood home in New York. At that time, it was the custom for entire families to be buried next to each other. Rich families built stone crypts to hold them.

Caroline's family was rich. A stone crypt waited for her and her baby. After the funeral, her husband shipped their bodies back to New

York. Caroline's casket was different from most coffins, which were made of wood. Hers was an iron casket with a glass face plate. Once she was placed inside, the coffin was hermetically sealed. This meant air could not enter the coffin. And no oxygen meant no decay. Because of this, Caroline's family and friends in New York could say goodbye to the girl they loved. Since there was no deterioration, Caroline would look exactly as she had when they last saw her.

Caroline's iron coffin lay undisturbed in the Sutherland Crypt for eighty years.

That's when a local boy stumbled upon Caroline. Perhaps he shouldn't have been prowling around a graveyard, but he was curious and probably looking for adventure. He was poking around the cemetery when he saw a stone crypt. Everyone knew what crypts held, so no one was surprised the boy thought it might be spooky and fun to peek inside it. He was brave but also very foolish.

The wooden door to the crypt had crumbled over the years. It was easy for the boy to pull on the latch. When he did, the door fell open for him. Inside, he saw two deteriorating wood coffins: a baby-sized bronze coffin, and an odd iron coffin. He had never seen one before, so clearly, he had to investigate.

(What budding ghost hunter WOULDN'T?)

A thick layer of dust lay across the glass

plate of the iron coffin. The boy had never seen anything like that. Curious, he wiped the dust away and found himself face-to-face with Caroline!

But . . . she didn't *look* like a corpse. Instead, he saw a lovely young woman, seemingly asleep, holding a perfect white rose. It didn't take long for the townspeople to come see for themselves. How could a woman, buried eighty years ago, still look so beautiful?

The crypt was resealed, but that didn't stop the curious. Three times, people broke into the crypt. The third time, unfortunately, someone cracked the glass face plate. "That was that," your dad says. "It wasn't long before Caroline and her snow-white rose crumbled into dust."

Your mom says there is one final thing she wants to do. Catskills locals told her that if she walked the fields and the cemetery, she might catch a glimpse of Caroline in her white dress.

Because apparently . . . Caroline doesn't know she's dead.

Unfortunately, it's not June 13. That's the day of Caroline's wedding and the best time to see her ghost. Still, you scan the fields until it's time to go. Once, you think you see something, but when you look again, it is gone. Could it have been a scarecrow?

Maybe.

Or maybe you saw Caroline, walking the very same fields she did as a girl, a white flower in her hand.

You've had an adventure in the Catskills. It hasn't been a typical trip, where you hike, bike, canoe, and mountain climb. It's not the trip your grandparents might have taken, for you don't stay in resorts with standup comedians or Big Band orchestras.

The Catskills *you've* seen is full of ghosts, witches, and even a headless horseman. You visited in the last days of fall, and you saw red and gold forests, pumpkin fields, and quaint bed and breakfasts. You've sat by a cozy fire, sipped apple cider, and drifted off to sleep in comfy chairs. Not to mention gotten to ride a snowmobile!

Maybe even you, dear reader, will dream of the restless ghosts that roam the Catskills. You've met some of them in this book. It's easy to see more. Just book an airline ticket or get in your car, and soon, you'll find yourself living another spooky tale, courtesy of the Catskills.

Karen Miller has been writing about strange creatures since she was six, so writing about the paranormal is a perfect fit. She just moved to Iowa City and is excited to meet those ghosts.

Check out some of the other *Spooky America* titles available now!

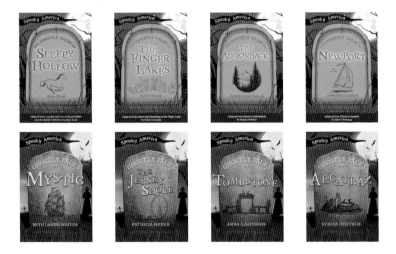

Spooky America was adapted from the creeptastic *Haunted America* series for adults. *Haunted America* explores historical haunts in cities and regions across America. Here's more from the original *Haunted Catskills* author Lisa LaMonica: